Sustainable Solopreneurship

SUFI

Sustainable Solopreneurship

CONTENT..1
Introduction 5
1 9
2 13
3 18
4 23
5 28
6 33
7 38
8 43
9 48
Conclusion 53
NOTES 56
AUTHOR..61

1.
2.
3.
4.
5.
6.
7.
8.
9.
10.
11.
12.
13.

Chapter 1

CONTENT

Chapter 1: The Solopreneur's Unique Challenge in a Sustainable World

- 1.1 Why Solopreneurs Are Uniquely Positioned to Lead Sustainability
- 1.2 The Balance Between Profit, Purpose, and Environmental Responsibility
- 1.3 Common Challenges Solopreneurs Face in Implementing Sustainability
- 1.4 Case Study: A Solopreneur's Journey to Sustainability
- 1.5 Exercise: Identifying Your Sustainability Challenges and Opportunities

Chapter 2: Setting the Foundation for a Sustainable Business

- 2.1 The Triple Bottom Line: People, Planet, and Profit
- 2.2 Conducting a Sustainability Audit
    - 2.2.1 Assessing Your Environmental Impact
    - 2.2.2 Evaluating Financial Sustainability
    - 2.2.3 Social Impact: How Your Business Affects Communities
- 2.3 SMART Sustainability Goals: A Framework for Action
- 2.4 Case Study: Creating a 6-Month Action Plan for a Freelance Business

- 2.5 Exercise: Creating Your Business's Sustainability Action Plan

Chapter 3: Sustainable Sourcing and Ethical Supply Chains

- 3.1 What Is Sustainable Sourcing?
- 3.2 How to Evaluate Ethical Suppliers
- 3.3 Certifications That Ensure Sustainability (Fair Trade, Organic, etc.)
- 3.4 Case Study: A Solopreneur's Ethical Fashion Supply Chain
- 3.5 Exercise: Auditing Your Supply Chain for Sustainability

Chapter 4: Reducing Waste and Embracing Circular Economy Practices

- 4.1 What Is the Circular Economy?
- 4.2 How to Implement Waste Reduction Practices in Your Business
    - 4.2.1 Reducing Waste in Product-Based Businesses
    - 4.2.2 Service-Based Business Waste Reduction Tactics
- 4.3 Designing Products for Durability and Reuse
- 4.4 Case Study: Turning Waste into Resources with Upcycling
- 4.5 Exercise: Mapping Your Waste and Circular Economy Opportunities

Chapter 5: Energy Efficiency and Sustainable Business Practices

- 5.1 Why Energy Efficiency Is Crucial for Solopreneurs
- 5.2 Conducting an Energy Audit
    - 5.2.1 Identifying Energy Drains in Your Workspace

- ○ 5.2.2 Energy-Efficient Appliances and Devices
- 5.3 Renewable Energy Options for Small Businesses
- 5.4 Case Study: Lowering Energy Costs with Solar Panels
- 5.5 Exercise: Creating an Energy Efficiency Plan for Your Business

Chapter 6: Sustainable Marketing and Ethical Branding

- 6.1 What Is Sustainable Marketing?
- 6.2 Avoiding Greenwashing: Authenticity in Your Branding
- 6.3 How to Tell Your Sustainability Story
- 6.4 Case Study: An Eco-Friendly Business's Sustainable Marketing Strategy
- 6.5 Exercise: Developing Your Brand's Sustainability Message

Chapter 7: Sustainable Finance: Budgeting for a Greener Business

- 7.1 Understanding the Costs of Sustainability
- 7.2 Finding Cost-Effective Eco-Friendly Solutions
- 7.3 Calculating the Return on Investment (ROI) of Sustainable Practices
- 7.4 Case Study: A Solopreneur's Transition to Sustainable Finance
- 7.5 Exercise: Creating a Budget for Sustainability in Your Business

Chapter 8: Building Customer Loyalty Through Sustainability

- 8.1 Why Sustainability Drives Customer Loyalty
- 8.2 Creating a Green Loyalty Program

- 8.3 Engaging Eco-Conscious Consumers
- 8.4 Case Study: A Solopreneur's Eco-Friendly Engagement Strategy
- 8.5 Exercise: Designing a Customer Loyalty Program Centered Around Sustainability

Chapter 9: Long-Term Sustainability Planning for Solopreneurs

- 9.1 Setting Long-Term Sustainability Goals
- 9.2 Adapting to New Technologies and Innovations in Sustainability
- 9.3 Expanding Sustainability Practices as Your Business Grows
- 9.4 Case Study: A Solopreneur's Journey to Long-Term Sustainability
- 9.5 Exercise: Creating a 3-5 Year Sustainability Roadmap

Conclusion: Sustainability as the Future of Solopreneurship

- Key Takeaways and Final Thoughts
- Next Steps: Implementing What You've Learned
- Final Call to Action: Building a Sustainable Business for the Future

Chapter 2

Introduction

The Solopreneur's Path to Sustainability

As a solopreneur, you're not just running a business—you're wearing every hat, making every decision, and managing every aspect of your company. This level of independence is both empowering and challenging. While the flexibility to set your own hours and build your dream business is enticing, it often comes with intense pressure to juggle countless tasks, stay ahead of competitors, and—especially in today's climate—operate sustainably. In a world where sustainability is no longer just a buzzword but a vital business practice, solopreneurs are increasingly expected to embrace eco-conscious strategies without the large teams or resources that bigger companies rely on.

This book, *Sustainable Solopreneurship* , is designed to help you, the solo business owner, build a business that's not only profitable but also environmentally and socially responsible. More importantly, it offers practical, actionable steps that you can implement right away—even with limited resources or support. Whether you're just starting out or looking to make your existing business more sustainable, this guide will show you how to integrate sustainable practices that benefit both your business and the planet.

Why Sustainability Matters for Solopreneurs

Sustainability isn't just for big corporations. It's become a core value that **93% of global consumers** expect from businesses, according to a **Nielsen study** . More than ever, consumers are favoring companies that prioritize ethical sourcing, waste reduction, and environmental responsibility. For solopreneurs, this presents both a challenge and an opportunity. With sustainability at the forefront of consumer decision-making, integrating eco-friendly practices into your business can attract a loyal customer base, reduce costs, and position you as a leader in your industry.

But you might be thinking: "How can I implement sustainability when I'm already stretched thin, managing every part of the business myself?" The good news is that sustainability doesn't require massive overhauls or significant capital investments. Small, incremental changes—whether it's switching to eco-friendly packaging, reducing energy consumption, or sourcing sustainable materials—can have a significant impact on both your bottom line and your brand's reputation.

Case Study: The Sustainable Solopreneur Success of Laura Zabo

Consider the story of **Laura Zabo** , a solopreneur who turned her passion for sustainability into a thriving business. Laura's company creates fashion accessories from recycled bicycle tires, helping to reduce waste while creating unique, eco-friendly products. As a solopreneur, she not only runs the creative side of her business but also manages production, marketing, and customer service. Laura's commitment to sustainability has not only differentiated her brand in the crowded fashion industry but also earned her a loyal customer base that values ethical business practices. Her journey illustrates that with the right approach, sustainability can be a powerful tool for growth, even for solo entrepreneurs.

The Challenges of Sustainable Solopreneurship

However, it's important to acknowledge the unique challenges that solopreneurs face. Unlike larger companies, you don't have dedicated teams to handle marketing, product development, and customer service. Your time is split across multiple functions, making it easy to feel overwhelmed. Adding sustainability into the mix can feel like just another task on an already packed to-do list.

But what if sustainability could simplify your business instead of complicating it? By integrating sustainable practices into your operations, you can streamline processes, reduce costs, and create a business model that's built for longevity. In fact, many solopreneurs find that adopting sustainable practices helps them clarify their mission, attract purpose-driven customers, and build a brand that stands out from the competition.

What You'll Learn in This Book

Sustainable Solopreneurship is structured to guide you through every aspect of building and scaling a sustainable business as a solopreneur. Each chapter is designed to provide practical strategies, real-life case studies, and step-by-step action plans that you can immediately apply to your business.

Here's what you'll discover:

- **How to integrate sustainability into every part of your business** without overextending yourself.

- **Practical frameworks for reducing waste, energy use, and costs** while growing your business.

- **Real-life examples and case studies** from successful solopreneurs who have adopted eco-friendly practices and thrived.

- **How to leverage sustainability as a competitive advantage** , attracting customers who are passionate about supporting green businesses.

- **Step-by-step guides to creating a sustainable business model** , from product sourcing and packaging to ethical marketing and social responsibility.

Why This Book Will Work for You

This book isn't just about theory—it's about action. I've distilled years of research, case studies, and expert advice into a simple, approachable guide that's tailored specifically for solopreneurs. You won't find jargon or complex sustainability strategies that require large teams or hefty budgets. Instead, you'll get actionable advice that you can implement today to start making a difference for both your business and the environment.

Your Sustainable Journey Begins Now

The path to sustainable solopreneurship is not only achievable—it's essential. With consumers increasingly favoring companies that prioritize environmental responsibility, building a sustainable business is no longer just a nice-to-have; it's a competitive advantage. Whether you're looking to attract purpose-driven customers, reduce your environmental footprint, or build a long-lasting, purpose-driven business, this book will provide you with the tools and strategies you need to succeed.

So let's get started. Together, we'll explore how you can build a profitable, sustainable business that reflects your values and leaves a positive impact on the world. **Sustainable Solopreneurship** is not just a guide—it's your blueprint for thriving as a solo business owner in a world that values sustainability.

Chapter 3

1

The Solopreneur's Unique Challenge in a Sustainable World

1.1 Why Solopreneurs Are Uniquely Positioned to Lead Sustainability

Solopreneurs have a distinct advantage when it comes to implementing sustainability practices: their ability to make swift, intentional decisions. Unlike larger businesses with layers of bureaucracy, solopreneurs can pivot quickly, test eco-friendly practices, and integrate them into their business models without waiting for approval from higher-ups or departments. This flexibility gives them an edge in adopting **green practices** and responding to consumer demands for sustainability.

However, solopreneurs also face the challenge of balancing sustainability with profitability. Sustainability is often seen as a long-term investment, and it can feel daunting for a small, one-person business to take on eco-friendly initiatives when financial resources are already stretched. Despite these challenges, solopreneurs can lead the way by starting small and scaling their efforts gradually, showing that it's possible to build both a sustainable and profitable business.

1.2 The Balance Between Profit, Purpose, and Environmental Responsibility

In the solopreneur world, striking a balance between **profit** and **purpose** is vital. Today's consumers are not just looking for great products or services—they want to support businesses that align with their values. According to a **Nielsen study**, **73% of global consumers** are willing to change their consumption habits to reduce their environmental impact. For solopreneurs, this means that integrating sustainability can enhance your brand's appeal, driving both **customer loyalty** and **long-term profitability**.

This balance starts with understanding the **triple bottom line** : People, Planet, and Profit. Traditionally, businesses have focused on profit maximization, often at the expense of social and environmental factors. But in the modern marketplace, businesses that ignore their impact on people and the planet are increasingly at risk of losing customers and credibility.

Solopreneurs can start by adopting small, cost-effective sustainability initiatives, such as reducing waste or switching to **eco-friendly suppliers** . These changes not only reduce environmental harm but can also lead to significant cost savings over time, especially in areas like energy use and packaging.

1.3 Common Challenges Solopreneurs Face in Implementing Sustainability

While solopreneurs are well-positioned to integrate sustainable practices, they also face several challenges:

- **Limited Resources** : As a one-person operation, solopreneurs often lack the financial and human resources that larger businesses have access to. This can make it difficult to invest in **eco-friendly products** or processes that may have a higher upfront cost.

- **Lack of Time** : Solopreneurs juggle multiple roles—CEO, marketing manager, customer service rep, and more. This can leave little time for researching or implementing sustainable practices.

- **Information Overload** : With so much information available about sustainability, it can be overwhelming to know where to start. Solopreneurs may struggle to identify which practices will have the most impact on their business and how to integrate them effectively.

Despite these challenges, solopreneurs can overcome them by focusing on small, achievable changes that lead to long-term benefits. For instance, starting with a **waste**

reduction strategy or switching to **energy-efficient office equipment** can make a significant impact without requiring a large investment of time or money.

1.4 Case Study: A Solopreneur's Journey to Sustainability

Take the case of *Lisa* , a solopreneur who runs a small business creating handmade jewelry. Initially, she focused solely on profit, using inexpensive materials to keep her costs low. However, as customer demand for sustainable products grew, Lisa realized that her business could benefit from aligning with eco-friendly values. She began researching ways to source recycled metals and ethical gemstones and switched to eco-friendly packaging.

At first, Lisa was concerned that the higher costs of sustainable materials would cut into her profit margins. However, as she began marketing her business as **eco-conscious** , she attracted a new segment of customers who valued her commitment to sustainability. These customers were willing to pay a premium for her products because they aligned with their values, allowing Lisa to maintain profitability while reducing her business's environmental footprint.

By integrating sustainability into her business model, Lisa not only enhanced her brand but also built a loyal customer base that appreciated her dedication to ethical practices.

1.5 Exercise: Identifying Your Sustainability Challenges and Opportunities

Now it's your turn to reflect on your own business. What challenges are preventing you from integrating sustainability? And where are the opportunities for improvement?

Take a few minutes to answer the following questions:

1. **What are my business's most significant environmental impacts?** (e.g., energy use, materials, packaging, transportation)
2. **What small, cost-effective changes can I make today to reduce my impact?** (e.g., switching to recycled materials, reducing energy consumption)

3. **What areas of my business are most aligned with sustainability trends?** (e.g., eco-friendly products, social impact initiatives)

4. **What are the long-term opportunities for integrating sustainability into my business model?** (e.g., partnerships with ethical suppliers, customer engagement through green initiatives)

By identifying these areas, you can start to develop a sustainability action plan that aligns with your business's goals and resources. Even small changes can lead to big impacts, both for the environment and your bottom line.

This chapter provides an overview of the challenges and opportunities solopreneurs face when integrating sustainability into their businesses. By exploring real-world examples, like Lisa's jewelry business, and engaging in self-reflection exercises, solopreneurs can begin their journey toward creating a business that balances **profit** with **purpose** and **planet**.

Chapter 4

2

Setting the Foundation for a Sustainable Business

2.1 The Triple Bottom Line: People, Planet, and Profit

The **Triple Bottom Line (TBL)** is a sustainability framework that encourages businesses to consider three dimensions of performance: **social** (people), **environmental** (planet), and **economic** (profit). This approach contrasts with traditional business models, which focus solely on profitability. As a solopreneur, you are in a unique position to incorporate this framework early in your business, ensuring that sustainability is embedded in the core of your operations from the beginning.

1. People : The social aspect of TBL focuses on the impact your business has on employees, customers, suppliers, and the community. For solopreneurs, this could mean ensuring ethical sourcing practices, offering fair pricing, and engaging with your customers in meaningful ways. Your business can also play a role in uplifting underrepresented communities through your work.

2. Planet : The environmental aspect looks at how your business interacts with the natural world. Solopreneurs can reduce their ecological footprint by adopting eco-friendly practices such as using sustainable materials, reducing waste, and conserving energy. A commitment to protecting the planet not only improves your brand image but also reduces costs in the long run.

3. Profit : Economic sustainability is crucial for your business's longevity. It's about making a profit without sacrificing social and environmental values. While some sustainable practices may have upfront costs, they often lead to long-term financial benefits, such as customer loyalty, operational efficiencies, and brand differentiation.

2.2 Conducting a Sustainability Audit

Before making any changes, it's important to understand where your business currently stands in terms of sustainability. A **sustainability audit** helps you assess your current practices, identify areas for improvement, and set realistic goals for the future.

2.2.1 Assessing Your Environmental Impact

The first step is to evaluate how your business impacts the environment. This includes energy usage, waste generation, transportation, and product sourcing. Start by asking the following questions:

- How much energy does my business use, and can I reduce it through energy-efficient technologies or renewable energy?
- What waste is my business generating, and how can I minimize it through recycling or reducing packaging?
- Are the materials I'm using sustainably sourced?

2.2.2 Evaluating Financial Sustainability

Next, consider how your business finances align with sustainability. Are you investing in eco-friendly practices that could save money over time? For example, switching to energy-efficient appliances might require an initial investment but could lead to significant savings on electricity bills. Financial sustainability also means ensuring that your business is profitable enough to grow while maintaining ethical and eco-friendly practices.

2.2.3 Social Impact: How Your Business Affects Communities

Finally, assess the social impact of your business. Are you contributing positively to the community or supporting fair labor practices? Do you offer value to your customers and suppliers beyond transactions, such as through educational content or ethical practices? Evaluating your social impact can help build stronger relationships with customers who care about your values.

2.3 SMART Sustainability Goals: A Framework for Action

After completing your sustainability audit, it's time to set goals. Using the **SMART** framework ensures that your goals are clear and achievable:

- **Specific** : Clearly define what you want to achieve. For example, "reduce energy consumption by 20%."
- **Measurable** : Set criteria to track progress. For instance, measure energy usage before and after implementing changes.
- **Achievable** : Ensure your goals are realistic based on your resources.
- **Relevant** : Focus on goals that align with your overall business strategy and values.
- **Time-bound** : Set a deadline for achieving each goal, such as reducing waste by 10% within 6 months.

Example of a SMART Goal : "Switch to 100% recycled packaging within the next three months by sourcing from local suppliers."

2.4 Case Study: Creating a 6-Month Action Plan for a Freelance Business

Let's take the example of *Rachel* , a freelance graphic designer who wanted to reduce her environmental impact while maintaining profitability. After conducting a sustainability audit, Rachel found that her biggest environmental impact came from printing materials and energy consumption.

Using the **SMART** framework, she set the following goals:

1. **Reduce energy consumption by 15%** by switching to LED lighting and powering down her computer at night.
2. **Switch to 100% recycled paper** for client presentations and marketing materials within 3 months.

3. **Go paperless for client invoicing** by transitioning to digital invoices and contracts within 6 months.

Rachel's goals were specific and measurable, and she used her 6-month timeline to gradually implement changes without disrupting her workflow. By the end of the six months, Rachel had not only reduced her carbon footprint but also saved money on energy bills and printing costs. She also promoted her eco-friendly changes to her clients, which helped attract more business from like-minded companies.

2.5 Exercise: Creating Your Business's Sustainability Action Plan

Now it's your turn to create a sustainability action plan for your business. Using the SMART framework, identify three specific sustainability goals that you can implement in the next 6-12 months.

1. **Goal 1** : Write down a specific, measurable goal related to **energy efficiency** (e.g., reduce electricity consumption, switch to renewable energy sources).
2. **Goal 2** : Identify a **waste reduction** goal (e.g., reduce packaging waste, implement a recycling program).
3. **Goal 3** : Set a goal focused on **social impact** (e.g., sourcing from ethical suppliers, contributing to community initiatives).

Once you've written down your goals, outline a timeline and the steps needed to achieve each one. Start with small, achievable changes and build up as your business grows.

Conclusion of Chapter 2

By setting a strong foundation for sustainability, you are positioning your business for long-term success. The **Triple Bottom Line** framework ensures that you're not just focusing on profit but also on the impact your business has on people and the planet. Conducting a **sustainability audit** helps you understand your starting point, and setting **SMART goals** ensures that your path forward is both realistic and impactful. With a clear plan in place, you can confidently begin your journey toward a more sustainable business model.

Chapter 5

3

Sustainable Sourcing and Ethical Supply Chains

In this chapter, we will explore the importance of **sustainable sourcing** and building **ethical supply chains** as a solopreneur. These two components are essential for reducing your business's environmental impact, building trust with customers, and aligning your brand with eco-conscious values.

3.1 What Is Sustainable Sourcing?

Sustainable sourcing involves choosing materials, products, and services that are produced in a way that respects both people and the planet. It's about making conscious decisions to minimize environmental harm and support ethical labor practices. Sustainable sourcing looks at the entire supply chain—from the raw materials used to how those materials are transformed into finished products.

As a solopreneur, your ability to source sustainably is a key competitive advantage. Whether you're selling physical products, offering digital services, or running a consultancy, choosing sustainable options for the resources you use is an opportunity to create a positive impact.

Key considerations for sustainable sourcing include:

- **Renewability** : Are the materials you're using renewable or non-renewable? Can they be replenished naturally without depleting resources?
- **Recycled Materials** : Can you use recycled materials in your products or packaging to reduce waste?
- **Local Sourcing** : Are you supporting local businesses to reduce the carbon footprint associated with shipping?

- **Ethical Labor Practices** : Are your suppliers paying fair wages and ensuring safe working conditions?

3.2 How to Evaluate Ethical Suppliers

Finding suppliers who align with your values is crucial for building an ethical supply chain. The goal is to ensure that every step of your supply chain reflects your commitment to sustainability and ethical business practices.

Here are steps to evaluate your suppliers:

1. **Research Supplier Practices** : Investigate the supplier's practices, focusing on how they source their materials, treat their workers, and manage their environmental impact. Suppliers that are transparent about their processes tend to be more reliable.

2. **Ask for Certifications** : Look for certifications that verify the sustainability and ethics of a supplier's operations. Common certifications include:
   - **Fair Trade** : Ensures that producers receive fair wages and work in safe conditions.
   - **USDA Organic** : Indicates that products are produced using organic methods, free from synthetic pesticides and fertilizers.
   - **Forest Stewardship Council (FSC)** : Guarantees that wood and paper products come from responsibly managed forests.

3. **Check for Environmental Initiatives** : Suppliers should be implementing measures to reduce their environmental footprint. This could include reducing water and energy consumption, using renewable energy, or managing waste responsibly.

4. **Request Supply Chain Transparency** : Ethical suppliers will be willing to share details about their sourcing, production methods, and environmental policies.

Transparency ensures that you know exactly where your materials are coming from and how they are produced.

3.3 Certifications That Ensure Sustainability (Fair Trade, Organic, etc.)

Choosing suppliers with the right certifications can give your business credibility and ensure that your sourcing aligns with your sustainability goals. Some of the most recognized certifications are:

1. **Fair Trade Certification** : This certification guarantees that products are made with fair labor practices, ensuring that workers are paid fair wages, work in safe conditions, and have access to benefits. It's especially important for businesses that rely on international suppliers.

2. **USDA Organic Certification** : If your business involves food products, ingredients, or textiles like cotton, the USDA Organic label ensures that the products are grown without synthetic pesticides, herbicides, or fertilizers, and are GMO-free.

3. **Forest Stewardship Council (FSC) Certification** : The FSC label on wood, paper, and other forest-based products ensures that these materials come from sustainably managed forests. For solopreneurs using packaging, printing, or wooden products, this is an important label to look for.

4. **B Corporation Certification** : B Corp certification is awarded to companies that meet the highest standards of social and environmental performance, accountability, and transparency. While it's more common for larger businesses, some solopreneurs may benefit from the credibility and trust it offers.

5. **Cradle to Cradle Certification** : This certification evaluates the entire lifecycle of a product, ensuring that it is safe, circular, and responsibly produced. Cradle to Cradle principles focus on reducing waste and designing products for reuse or recycling.

3.4 Case Study: A Solopreneur's Ethical Fashion Supply Chain

Emma, a solopreneur running a small eco-friendly clothing brand, realized that to align with her brand's values, she needed to make changes to her supply chain. Initially, she used conventional cotton, but after learning about the negative environmental impact of conventional cotton farming (high water use, pesticide pollution), she decided to switch to organic cotton certified by the Global Organic Textile Standard (GOTS).

Emma also researched her supply chain to ensure that the workers who produced her fabrics were treated fairly. She partnered with a Fair Trade-certified textile factory that guaranteed safe working conditions and fair wages. By aligning her supply chain with her values, Emma not only reduced her environmental footprint but also built a brand that resonated with eco-conscious consumers. Her transparency about her sourcing practices attracted loyal customers who were willing to pay a premium for ethically produced products.

3.5 Exercise: Auditing Your Supply Chain for Sustainability

Now that you understand the importance of sustainable sourcing, it's time to evaluate your own supply chain. Follow these steps to audit your current suppliers and identify areas for improvement:

1. **List Your Current Suppliers** : Write down all of the suppliers or vendors you currently work with, including those providing materials, products, or services.

2. **Evaluate Their Practices** :
    - Do they have any sustainability certifications (e.g., Fair Trade, FSC, Organic)?
    - Are they transparent about their sourcing practices?
    - Do they offer recycled, renewable, or ethically sourced materials?

3. **Set Improvement Goals** : Based on your findings, set goals for improving your supply chain. For example, you could switch to a supplier that offers recycled materials or find a vendor closer to home to reduce transportation emissions.

4. **Contact Suppliers for More Information** : If you're unsure about your suppliers' practices, reach out to them. Ask about their sustainability initiatives and whether they can provide more environmentally friendly options.

Conclusion of Chapter 3

Sustainable sourcing and building an ethical supply chain are critical steps toward creating a truly eco-friendly business. As a solopreneur, these decisions can differentiate your brand, reduce environmental impact, and build customer trust. By carefully evaluating suppliers, choosing those with the right certifications, and ensuring that your products are ethically sourced, you are taking the necessary steps to align your business with sustainability goals.

Chapter 6

4

Reducing Waste and Embracing Circular Economy Practices

Waste is one of the most visible signs of unsustainable business practices, and solopreneurs—despite their small scale—play a crucial role in minimizing waste. Whether it's excess packaging, energy inefficiency, or discarded materials, waste reduction not only benefits the planet but also cuts down costs, creating more efficient, profitable business models. One of the most effective ways to minimize waste is by embracing the principles of the **circular economy**, which aims to reduce waste through reuse, recycling, and designing products with longer lifecycles.

4.1 What Is the Circular Economy?

The **circular economy** is a model of production and consumption that focuses on extending the life of products and materials, thus minimizing waste. In contrast to the traditional "take, make, dispose" linear model, the circular economy promotes practices such as:

- **Designing out waste** : Creating products that are durable, repairable, and recyclable.
- **Keeping products in use** : Encouraging reuse, repair, refurbishing, and recycling to extend the lifecycle of goods.
- **Regenerating natural systems** : Ensuring that materials are used in a way that can replenish ecosystems, rather than depleting them.

The goal of the circular economy is to move away from disposable products and embrace a regenerative approach that benefits businesses, society, and the environment. For solopreneurs, this model not only reduces costs but also builds trust with consumers who are increasingly seeking out businesses that prioritize sustainability.

4.2 How to Implement Waste Reduction Practices in Your Business

There are several practical steps you can take to reduce waste, regardless of the size of your business or the industry you operate in. By focusing on efficient resource use and minimizing waste, you can save money, enhance your brand reputation, and contribute to environmental preservation.

4.2.1 Reducing Waste in Product-Based Businesses

If you run a business that manufactures or sells physical products, waste can occur at various stages of the production and distribution process. Here's how to tackle it:

1. **Eco-Friendly Packaging** : Replace traditional, wasteful packaging with sustainable alternatives. Use recycled materials, biodegradable options like cardboard and compostable plastics, or minimal packaging designs. By reducing excess packaging, you not only cut down on waste but also save money on materials.

2. **Design for Durability** : Instead of designing products that wear out quickly and need to be replaced, focus on creating high-quality, durable goods that can withstand the test of time. This reduces waste in the long term by keeping products in use longer.

3. **Product Returns and Repairs** : Offer repair services or incentives for customers to return products for refurbishing or recycling. This helps keep your products in circulation longer, reducing waste and contributing to a circular economy model.

4.2.2 Service-Based Business Waste Reduction Tactics

Even service-based businesses can reduce waste by making small, impactful changes:

1. **Go Paperless** : One of the easiest ways to reduce waste in a service-based business is by switching to digital documents, contracts, and invoices. Tools like **DocuSign** ,

Google Drive, or **Dropbox** can help keep your paperwork digital and accessible while minimizing paper waste.

2. **Energy-Efficient Technology** : Invest in energy-efficient technology, such as laptops, lighting, and office equipment, to reduce energy waste. Devices with **Energy Star** certification consume less energy, which also lowers your operational costs over time.

3. **Digital Communication** : Instead of relying on printed marketing materials, shift to digital marketing strategies, such as email newsletters, social media, and online advertising, which are not only more sustainable but also more cost-effective.

4.3 Designing Products for Durability and Reuse

A key principle of the circular economy is to design products with longevity and reuse in mind. By focusing on durable materials and modular designs, you can ensure that your products stay in use longer and don't end up in landfills after a single use. Here's how to get started:

1. **Use High-Quality Materials** : Choose materials that are durable, repairable, and recyclable. For example, instead of using cheap plastics that degrade quickly, opt for materials like stainless steel, aluminum, or recycled plastics that are built to last.

2. **Modular Design** : Consider creating products with parts that can be easily repaired or replaced. This encourages consumers to fix products rather than discard them when something breaks. Modular designs also make it easier to recycle parts once the product reaches the end of its useful life.

3. **Product-as-a-Service** : Instead of selling products outright, you can offer a product-as-a-service model, where customers rent or lease items and return them for repair or replacement when needed. This model works well for high-value items

such as electronics, tools, or equipment and ensures that products stay in circulation rather than being discarded after use.

4.4 Case Study: Turning Waste into Resources with Upcycling

Ben , a solopreneur in the home décor business, built his brand around upcycling discarded materials. He sourced wood from old shipping pallets and metal from scrap yards, transforming these into unique, handcrafted furniture pieces. By using materials that would otherwise be thrown away, Ben drastically reduced his raw material costs and positioned his business as eco-friendly and innovative.

Not only did Ben's upcycled products resonate with environmentally conscious customers, but his waste-reduction efforts also created a strong narrative for his brand. Customers were willing to pay a premium for his sustainable, one-of-a-kind products, allowing him to grow his business while maintaining his commitment to sustainability.

4.5 Exercise: Mapping Your Waste and Circular Economy Opportunities

Now it's time to apply these principles to your own business. Take a moment to map out the waste generated by your business and identify areas where you can implement circular economy practices.

1. **List the Waste Your Business Produces** : Break this down by category, such as packaging, energy, materials, or office supplies.
2. **Identify Opportunities for Reduction** :
    - Can you reduce packaging or switch to more sustainable materials?
    - Is there an opportunity to reuse or recycle waste materials?
    - Can you design products to be more durable or modular?
3. **Create a Waste Reduction Action Plan** : Based on your list, identify at least three specific changes you can make to reduce waste and embrace circular economy

practices. Set a timeline for implementing these changes and measure your progress over time.

Conclusion of Chapter 4

Reducing waste is not only an environmental imperative but also a sound business strategy for solopreneurs. By adopting the principles of the **circular economy**, you can minimize your environmental impact, reduce costs, and differentiate your brand in an increasingly eco-conscious marketplace. Whether you're designing products to last, upcycling materials, or reducing packaging waste, these small but significant changes will help your business thrive sustainably.

Chapter 7

5

Energy Efficiency and Sustainable Business Practices

Energy efficiency is a key aspect of sustainability for solopreneurs. Reducing energy consumption not only minimizes your environmental impact but also leads to significant cost savings. By adopting sustainable business practices, you can optimize how your business uses energy and contribute to a greener future, all while maintaining or even improving your business's profitability.

In this chapter, we'll explore practical energy-efficient strategies, discuss the benefits of renewable energy options, and offer actionable steps for solopreneurs looking to implement sustainable business practices.

5.1 Why Energy Efficiency Is Crucial for Solopreneurs

Energy consumption is one of the most significant contributors to carbon emissions. According to the **International Energy Agency (IEA)**, energy-related carbon emissions accounted for nearly **60% of total global greenhouse gas emissions** in recent years. Solopreneurs, like larger businesses, can help reduce this impact by adopting energy-efficient practices.

Here's why energy efficiency should be a priority for your business:

1. **Cost Savings** : Reducing energy consumption leads to lower utility bills. Even small changes, such as switching to energy-efficient appliances or optimizing office lighting, can lead to significant savings over time.

2. **Environmental Responsibility** : Solopreneurs play a role in global sustainability efforts. By reducing energy usage, you are helping decrease carbon

emissions, reduce the demand for non-renewable energy sources, and contribute to a cleaner planet.

3. **Customer Appeal** : More consumers are supporting eco-conscious businesses. According to **Nielsen** , nearly **66% of global consumers** are willing to pay more for products from businesses that are committed to environmental sustainability. By improving your energy efficiency, you can appeal to this growing market of eco-conscious customers.

5.2 Conducting an Energy Audit

Before making energy-efficient changes, it's important to first assess how much energy your business consumes and identify areas for improvement. A simple **energy audit** helps you track usage, pinpoint inefficiencies, and discover opportunities to reduce energy waste.

5.2.1 Identifying Energy Drains in Your Workspace

Here's how you can begin your energy audit:

1. **Monitor Energy Usage** : Use a smart meter or energy-tracking device to measure how much energy your business consumes daily. This data will help you understand patterns in your energy usage.

2. **Identify High-Energy Devices** : Certain appliances and devices use more energy than others. Laptops, desktop computers, printers, lighting, and heating/cooling systems are common culprits. Focus on these areas when considering upgrades or efficiency strategies.

3. **Look for "Phantom" Energy Use** : Phantom energy refers to the electricity consumed by devices that are plugged in but not in use. Items like chargers, printers, or computers continue to draw power even when turned off. Using **smart power strips** can automatically cut off energy when devices aren't in use, reducing phantom energy drain.

5.2.2 Energy-Efficient Appliances and Devices

Once you've identified where energy is being consumed, it's time to implement solutions. One of the most effective ways to reduce energy consumption is by upgrading to **Energy Star-certified appliances** . These appliances use significantly less energy compared to traditional devices.

Here are some devices worth upgrading for energy savings:

- **Energy-Efficient Lighting** : Switching to **LED bulbs** can reduce lighting energy use by up to **75%** compared to incandescent bulbs.
- **Laptops vs. Desktops** : Laptops generally consume up to **80% less energy** than desktop computers. If your work doesn't require high processing power, consider switching to a laptop.
- **Programmable Thermostats** : In offices or home workspaces that require heating or cooling, **programmable thermostats** can help you regulate temperature more efficiently, saving energy by adjusting temperatures based on the time of day.

5.3 Renewable Energy Options for Small Businesses

While reducing your energy consumption is crucial, switching to **renewable energy** is an even more impactful step toward sustainability. By powering your business with renewable energy sources like solar, wind, or hydropower, you can significantly reduce your carbon footprint.

1. Solar Power

For solopreneurs who own their workspace or home office, **solar panels** are an excellent long-term investment. While the initial installation cost can be high, many governments offer **tax incentives** and rebates for businesses that invest in solar energy. Over time, solar power can drastically reduce or even eliminate your electricity costs.

2. Green Energy Providers

If installing solar panels isn't feasible, consider switching to a **green energy plan** through your utility provider. Many electricity companies now offer options to source some or all of your energy from renewable sources like wind or solar farms.

3. Renewable Energy Credits (RECs)

For solopreneurs who cannot directly use renewable energy, purchasing **Renewable Energy Credits (RECs)** is another way to offset energy consumption. RECs allow businesses to support renewable energy projects, such as wind farms or solar plants, by purchasing credits equivalent to their energy use.

5.4 Case Study: Lowering Energy Costs with Solar Panels

Oliver, a freelance web designer, worked out of his home office and relied heavily on his computer equipment and lighting for long hours each day. Concerned about both his electricity bills and his carbon footprint, Oliver decided to invest in a small set of **solar panels** for his home office.

While the upfront cost was substantial, Oliver took advantage of a **government tax rebate** for solar installations, which covered **30% of the installation cost** . After the panels were up and running, Oliver noticed a significant drop in his monthly electricity bills—down by nearly **60%** . Over the next few years, Oliver was able to pay off the initial investment with the savings he made on energy, all while operating a nearly carbon-neutral business.

5.5 Exercise: Creating an Energy Efficiency Plan for Your Business

Now that you've learned the benefits of energy efficiency and renewable energy, it's time to create your own **Energy Efficiency Plan** . Follow these steps to start implementing changes:

1. **Conduct an Energy Audit** : Use the steps from section 5.2 to audit your current energy usage. Identify high-energy devices and areas of inefficiency.

2. **Set a Goal** : Based on your audit, set a specific energy reduction goal (e.g., reduce energy consumption by **20%** within the next year).

3. **Upgrade Appliances** : List at least three appliances or devices you can upgrade to more energy-efficient models.

4. **Consider Renewable Energy** : Research whether solar panels or green energy options are feasible for your business. If not, look into purchasing Renewable Energy Credits to offset your energy use.

5. **Track Your Progress** : Use energy tracking tools or your utility bills to monitor your progress and measure the impact of the changes you make.

Conclusion of Chapter 5

Adopting energy-efficient practices and exploring renewable energy options are vital steps for solopreneurs who want to build sustainable, eco-conscious businesses. By conducting an energy audit, upgrading to energy-efficient devices, and considering renewable energy, you'll reduce your environmental impact and enjoy long-term cost savings.

Chapter 8

6

Sustainable Marketing and Ethical Branding

Sustainability isn't just about what you do—it's also about how you communicate your values to the world. As a solopreneur, building a brand that reflects your commitment to sustainability is crucial to attracting customers who share those values. **Sustainable marketing** involves authentically promoting your eco-friendly practices, while **ethical branding** ensures that you're honest, transparent, and committed to long-term positive impact. In this chapter, we'll explore how you can effectively communicate your sustainability efforts without falling into the trap of greenwashing, and we'll provide actionable strategies to market your brand ethically.

6.1 What Is Sustainable Marketing?

Sustainable marketing is the process of promoting products or services in a way that highlights their environmental and social benefits. For solopreneurs, it's about weaving sustainability into the core of your marketing strategy and making it clear to customers how your values align with theirs. It's not just about selling products; it's about **building a relationship** with your audience based on shared ethics and values.

Some key components of sustainable marketing include:

1. **Transparency** : Be open about your sustainability practices, including what you're doing well and areas where you're still improving.
2. **Consistency** : Make sure your marketing message aligns with your actual business practices. If your business claims to be eco-friendly, every aspect of your operation—from packaging to partnerships—should reflect that.

3. **Long-term Impact** : Sustainable marketing emphasizes long-term value over short-term sales. It focuses on creating products or services that contribute positively to society and the environment.

6.2 Avoiding Greenwashing: Authenticity in Your Branding

Greenwashing refers to the act of misleading consumers into believing a company's products or practices are more environmentally friendly than they actually are. This can severely damage a brand's reputation, especially in an era where customers are more educated and aware of greenwashing tactics.

To avoid greenwashing, solopreneurs should focus on:

1. **Being Honest** : If you're not 100% sustainable, be transparent about it. Customers appreciate honesty and the willingness to improve over time.

2. **Backing Up Claims** : Whenever you make a claim about sustainability (e.g., "100% recycled materials"), make sure you have the data or certifications to back it up. This builds trust and credibility.

3. **Highlighting Real Actions** : Rather than using vague terms like "eco-friendly" or "green," explain specific steps your business is taking. For example, "We reduced our energy consumption by 20% in the past year by switching to renewable energy."

Key Tactic : Use third-party certifications, such as **Fair Trade** , **USDA Organic** , or **B Corporation** , to validate your claims. These certifications ensure that your business adheres to recognized sustainability standards.

6.3 How to Tell Your Sustainability Story

Storytelling is one of the most powerful tools in sustainable marketing. It helps create an emotional connection with your audience and makes your sustainability efforts more relatable. By sharing your personal journey as a solopreneur, your challenges, and the actions you're taking to improve, you can engage your audience on a deeper level.

Here's how to tell your sustainability story effectively:

1. **Start with Your "Why"** : Why did you decide to make sustainability a core part of your business? Was there a specific moment or experience that inspired you? Share that with your audience.

2. **Share Your Journey** : Customers appreciate authenticity and transparency. Share the steps you've taken toward sustainability and the challenges you've faced. This can make your brand more human and relatable.

3. **Use Visuals** : Visual storytelling is particularly effective in digital marketing. Share photos or videos that show your sustainability practices in action—whether it's the eco-friendly materials you use, the packaging you've improved, or the renewable energy powering your business.

4. **Highlight Customer Involvement** : Encourage customers to be part of your sustainability journey. This could be through social media campaigns, testimonials from eco-conscious customers, or loyalty programs that reward sustainable behavior (e.g., discounts for returning used products for recycling).

6.4 Case Study: An Eco-Friendly Business's Sustainable Marketing Strategy

Clara , a solopreneur running a handmade skincare brand, built her entire marketing strategy around her commitment to sustainability. She started by ensuring that all her products were packaged in **recycled and biodegradable materials** , and she sourced ingredients from **certified organic farms** .

Clara was upfront with her customers about the challenges she faced, including the higher costs of sustainable ingredients and the difficulty in sourcing local materials. But rather than positioning these as negatives, she used them to reinforce her brand's commitment to quality and ethics. Clara also incorporated visual storytelling into her marketing, regularly sharing behind-the-scenes content on social media that showed her sustainable sourcing practices in action.

By engaging her audience with her honest, transparent journey, Clara built a strong community of loyal customers who valued her dedication to the planet. Her customers were more willing to pay premium prices for her products, knowing that they were contributing to a sustainable cause.

6.5 Exercise: Developing Your Brand's Sustainability Message

Take a moment to craft your own brand's sustainability message. Use the questions below to guide you:

1. **Why did you choose to integrate sustainability into your business?**
2. **What specific actions are you taking to reduce your environmental impact?** (e.g., using recycled materials, reducing energy consumption, supporting ethical labor practices)
3. **How does your sustainability journey reflect your values as a solopreneur?**
4. **What long-term impact do you want your business to have on the environment or society?**

Once you've answered these questions, draft a 3-4 sentence sustainability message that clearly communicates your commitment to sustainability. This message can be used on your website, in marketing materials, and on social media to help build your brand identity around eco-friendly values.

Conclusion of Chapter 6

Sustainable marketing and ethical branding go hand in hand when building a business that truly reflects your values as a solopreneur. By focusing on transparency, avoiding greenwashing, and crafting a compelling sustainability story, you can create a strong emotional connection with your customers while demonstrating your commitment to the environment. As you move forward, keep your branding and marketing efforts aligned with your sustainability goals, and remember that authenticity and honesty are the keys to building trust in an increasingly eco-conscious marketplace.

Chapter 9

7

Sustainable Finance: Budgeting for a Greener Business

Sustainability is often seen as an expensive or complicated venture for businesses, particularly for solopreneurs who are managing tight budgets. However, aligning your finances with sustainable practices doesn't have to break the bank. In fact, many sustainable practices can lead to long-term savings and provide a strong return on investment (ROI). In this chapter, we'll explore how solopreneurs can budget for a greener business, find cost-effective solutions, and calculate the long-term financial benefits of sustainable practices.

7.1 Understanding the Costs of Sustainability

Many solopreneurs hesitate to implement sustainable practices because they fear the upfront costs will outweigh the benefits. It's true that certain sustainable investments, such as renewable energy or eco-friendly materials, may have higher initial costs. However, the **long-term financial gains** often outweigh these early expenses.

Here are some common costs associated with sustainability:

1. **Switching to Sustainable Materials** : Sustainable materials like recycled paper, organic fabrics, or biodegradable plastics may cost more upfront than conventional materials.

2. **Energy-Efficient Upgrades** : Investing in energy-efficient appliances or solar panels can come with significant upfront costs, although these typically pay off over time through reduced energy bills.

3. **Certifications** : Obtaining sustainability certifications (such as **Fair Trade**, **B Corp**, or **USDA Organic**) involves upfront fees. While these can be expensive, they offer long-term value by building trust with consumers and giving your business a competitive edge.

Despite these costs, sustainable investments should be seen as opportunities to save money and enhance brand loyalty in the long run. **Sustainable businesses** often experience higher customer retention, improved efficiency, and reduced waste, all of which contribute to stronger financial outcomes over time.

7.2 Finding Cost-Effective Eco-Friendly Solutions

Sustainability doesn't always have to involve large investments. In fact, there are plenty of cost-effective ways to start integrating green practices into your business right away:

1. **Start Small** : If your budget is limited, start with small, affordable changes. For example, switch to **recycled paper** or opt for **biodegradable packaging**. These changes are relatively low-cost but can make a big impact on your business's environmental footprint.

2. **Energy Efficiency without High Costs** : Implement simple, energy-saving habits before investing in expensive upgrades. Use **LED lighting**, unplug devices when not in use, and minimize heating and cooling usage. You can also install **smart power strips** that reduce phantom energy consumption.

3. **Go Paperless** : Going digital is one of the most cost-effective sustainability measures. Use electronic contracts, invoices, and receipts to reduce paper usage. Cloud-based solutions, like **Google Drive**, **Notion**, or **DocuSign**, are affordable alternatives to physical documents.

4. **Outsource Sustainability** : If you can't afford to make certain sustainability changes in-house, consider outsourcing specific elements. For example, you can

partner with suppliers that already have sustainability certifications or third-party shipping companies that offer **carbon-neutral shipping**.

By making these smaller, more manageable changes, you can reduce costs while still contributing to a greener business model. As your budget grows, you can gradually invest in more significant sustainability initiatives.

7.3 Calculating the Return on Investment (ROI) of Sustainable Practices

When evaluating whether a sustainable investment is worthwhile, it's important to calculate the **return on investment (ROI)**. Sustainable practices often lead to cost savings over time, whether through reduced energy bills, lower waste management costs, or increased customer loyalty. Here's how to evaluate the ROI of your sustainability efforts:

1. Short-Term vs. Long-Term Savings

Sustainable practices like installing solar panels or switching to energy-efficient appliances typically have a **long-term payoff**. The initial investment may seem high, but the savings accrue over time as energy costs decrease and operational efficiency improves.

For example, if you spend $10,000 installing solar panels and save $2,000 per year on electricity, your investment will pay off in **five years**. After that, the energy savings contribute directly to your profit margin.

2. Waste Reduction and Cost Efficiency

By minimizing waste through more efficient use of resources, solopreneurs can reduce operational costs. For instance, using **recycled materials** can be cheaper than sourcing new materials in the long run. Additionally, reducing packaging waste or switching to **biodegradable** alternatives can save money by lowering disposal costs.

3. Increased Customer Loyalty and Willingness to Pay

Consumers are becoming increasingly loyal to brands that prioritize sustainability. According to **Nielsen**, **73% of global consumers** say they would definitely or probably change their consumption habits to reduce their environmental impact.

Customers are also willing to pay a premium for products from businesses they trust to be environmentally responsible.

4. Risk Mitigation

Sustainable businesses are better positioned to navigate future regulations, such as potential carbon taxes or stricter waste management laws. By adopting sustainability early, you reduce the risk of future compliance costs and stay ahead of industry trends.

7.4 Case Study: A Solopreneur's Transition to Sustainable Finance

Anna , a solopreneur running a small bakery, decided to switch to **organic ingredients** after conducting research on the environmental and health benefits. At first, she was concerned that the higher cost of organic flour, sugar, and dairy would make it difficult to maintain her margins. However, after making the switch, Anna noticed that her customer base began to grow, particularly among health-conscious and eco-minded consumers.

Anna also marketed her commitment to sustainability by using **biodegradable packaging** and offering discounts to customers who brought their own reusable containers. These changes resonated with her customers, and Anna was able to increase her prices slightly to cover the cost of organic ingredients without losing business. In the long run, the investment in sustainability not only boosted her sales but also helped differentiate her bakery from the competition.

7.5 Exercise: Creating a Budget for Sustainability in Your Business

Now that you understand the financial implications of sustainability, it's time to create a budget for incorporating eco-friendly practices into your business. Use the following steps to guide you:

1. **Identify Key Areas for Sustainability** : List areas of your business where you can integrate sustainable practices, such as materials sourcing, energy consumption, packaging, and waste management.

2. **Estimate Costs** : Research the costs of switching to more sustainable options. This could include the price difference between standard and organic ingredients, the cost of installing energy-efficient appliances, or the fees associated with sustainability certifications.

3. **Project Long-Term Savings** : Calculate the potential savings from your sustainable investments. This might include lower energy bills, reduced waste management costs, or increased customer loyalty and willingness to pay.

4. **Set a Realistic Budget** : Based on your cost estimates and projected savings, set a budget for implementing sustainable practices. Start with smaller changes if your budget is limited, and plan for larger investments as your business grows.

Conclusion of Chapter 7

Sustainable finance isn't just about managing costs—it's about making strategic investments that will benefit your business and the environment over the long term. By understanding the costs of sustainability, finding cost-effective solutions, and calculating the ROI of your efforts, you can create a greener, more profitable business. Whether you're making small adjustments to your daily operations or investing in renewable energy and sustainable materials, you're laying the foundation for a business that aligns with the values of today's eco-conscious consumers.

Chapter 10

8

Building Customer Loyalty Through Sustainability

In today's marketplace, **customer loyalty** is more than just a result of high-quality products or services; it is increasingly influenced by a brand's commitment to values such as sustainability, ethical practices, and social responsibility. As a solopreneur, you can use your business's sustainability efforts to not only attract customers but also retain them by building long-term relationships based on shared values. In this chapter, we'll explore how you can leverage your eco-friendly initiatives to build customer loyalty, create meaningful engagement, and grow a community of like-minded consumers.

8.1 Why Sustainability Drives Customer Loyalty

Consumers are becoming more conscious of the environmental impact of their purchases. According to a **Nielsen study**, **66% of global consumers** are willing to pay more for sustainable goods, and **73%** of millennials prefer to purchase from sustainable businesses. Customers today are not just looking for great products—they want to support businesses that align with their values, and sustainability is increasingly a key part of that equation.

Here's why sustainability drives loyalty:

1. **Values Alignment** : When customers share the same environmental and ethical values as a brand, they feel a deeper connection, which fosters loyalty. They are more likely to return to brands they trust to make a positive impact.

2. **Transparency and Trust** : Brands that are transparent about their sustainability practices and engage in **authentic marketing** gain consumer trust. Customers

appreciate businesses that are honest about their efforts—even if they're not perfect—and show commitment to continuous improvement.

3. **Community Engagement** : Sustainable businesses often create a sense of community among like-minded customers who care about their purchases' impact. This community engagement can foster deeper emotional connections and long-term loyalty.

8.2 Creating a Green Loyalty Program

One of the most effective ways to engage customers and reward their loyalty is by creating a **green loyalty program** . These programs incentivize customers to make eco-friendly choices, whether by returning products for recycling, purchasing sustainable products, or engaging in environmentally friendly behaviors.

Here are a few ideas for creating a green loyalty program:

1. **Reward Sustainable Behavior** : Offer points or discounts to customers who take part in sustainable actions, such as returning packaging for recycling, opting for digital receipts, or purchasing eco-friendly products.

2. **Incentivize Reuse** : Encourage customers to bring their own bags, containers, or packaging for in-store purchases or returns. Reward them with loyalty points, discounts, or exclusive offers when they reduce waste.

3. **Donate to Environmental Causes** : Allow customers to convert their loyalty points into donations to environmental charities or initiatives. This makes customers feel like they're contributing to a cause they care about through their loyalty to your brand.

4. **Exclusive Access** : Provide exclusive access to eco-friendly products, early releases of sustainable product lines, or educational content on sustainability for loyal customers.

Key Tactic : Personalize the program to reflect your brand's unique sustainability goals and ethos. The more aligned your loyalty program is with your core values, the more your customers will connect with it.

8.3 Engaging Eco-Conscious Consumers

Sustainability alone isn't enough to build customer loyalty—you need to **actively engage** with eco-conscious consumers. Engagement goes beyond simply offering products; it's about creating a two-way conversation with your customers and making them feel like they're part of your sustainability journey.

Here's how to effectively engage eco-conscious consumers:

1. **Educational Content** : Share informative content about sustainability, the environment, and the steps your business is taking to reduce its impact. Blog posts, social media updates, and videos explaining the benefits of your eco-friendly practices help customers understand your values and stay engaged.

2. **Involve Customers in Your Mission** : Ask for customer feedback on how you can improve your sustainability efforts or invite them to participate in local clean-up events, donation drives, or eco-friendly workshops. By involving your customers in these initiatives, you make them feel like partners in your mission.

3. **User-Generated Content** : Encourage your customers to share their experiences with your products and their own sustainability journeys. You can run social media campaigns that invite customers to share photos or stories about how they use your eco-friendly products in their daily lives.

4. **Transparent Reporting** : Keep customers informed about your sustainability milestones. Share updates about your progress in reducing waste, conserving energy, or sourcing ethical materials. Transparency builds trust and shows customers that your commitment to sustainability is genuine.

8.4 Case Study: A Solopreneur's Eco-Friendly Engagement Strategy

Mark, a solopreneur who runs a small eco-friendly coffee shop, wanted to build a loyal customer base that valued sustainability as much as he did. He started by implementing a **reusable cup discount program**, offering customers a small discount for bringing their own cups instead of using disposable ones. Over time, this initiative not only reduced waste but also became a key part of his shop's identity, attracting customers who shared his environmental values.

To deepen customer engagement, Mark created a **loyalty app** where customers could track their sustainability contributions, like how many disposable cups they had avoided by bringing their own. As customers accumulated points, they could exchange them for eco-friendly products in the shop, such as reusable straws or biodegradable cleaning products.

Mark also regularly posted updates on social media, sharing the collective impact his customers had made (e.g., "Together, we've saved 10,000 disposable cups from landfills!"). This engagement made customers feel like they were part of a community working toward a common goal, which increased their loyalty to Mark's coffee shop.

8.5 Exercise: Designing a Customer Loyalty Program Centered Around Sustainability

Now it's your turn to think about how you can design a loyalty program that encourages sustainability and rewards eco-conscious behavior. Use the steps below to create your own green loyalty program:

1. **Define Your Goals** : What sustainable behaviors do you want to encourage in your customers? For example, do you want to reduce waste, promote recycling, or encourage the purchase of eco-friendly products?

2. **Choose Your Incentives** : What rewards will you offer to loyal customers? This could include discounts, points, exclusive access to sustainable products, or donations to environmental causes.

3. **Create a Points System** : Develop a points-based system that rewards sustainable actions. For example, customers could earn points for returning packaging, purchasing eco-friendly products, or bringing their own bags or containers.

4. **Promote Your Program** : How will you introduce your loyalty program to customers? Plan a marketing campaign that highlights the benefits of participating and communicates your business's commitment to sustainability.

5. **Track and Share Progress** : Once the program is in place, track how many customers are participating and how much waste is being reduced. Share these milestones with your community to build a sense of collective achievement.

Conclusion of Chapter 8

Sustainability can be a powerful driver of customer loyalty when integrated into your business's marketing and engagement strategies. By creating a green loyalty program, actively involving customers in your mission, and using transparency and storytelling to communicate your progress, you can build long-term relationships with eco-conscious consumers. Solopreneurs have a unique opportunity to turn their sustainability initiatives into meaningful connections that not only retain customers but also contribute to the broader goal of a more sustainable world.

Chapter 11

9

Long-Term Sustainability Planning for Solopreneurs

Sustainability isn't just a one-time effort—it's a long-term commitment. As a solopreneur, the path toward building a sustainable business is ongoing, requiring you to constantly evolve and adapt to new environmental, social, and economic challenges. In this chapter, we'll focus on how to create a long-term sustainability plan that will help guide your business into the future. You'll learn how to set progressive goals, adapt to new technologies and innovations, and continuously improve your sustainability efforts as your business grows.

9.1 Setting Long-Term Sustainability Goals

A long-term sustainability plan requires setting ambitious but achievable goals that will guide your business through the next several years. These goals should be **measurable**, **impactful**, and aligned with your business's growth trajectory. While short-term goals may focus on making immediate changes like switching to recycled packaging, long-term goals should aim for deeper integration of sustainable practices that impact every area of your business.

Here's how to set effective long-term sustainability goals:

1. **Visionary Yet Practical** : Your goals should reflect the future you envision for your business. For example, committing to sourcing 100% renewable energy within five years or becoming a zero-waste business by a certain date is ambitious but achievable with planning.

2. **Break It Down** : Large sustainability goals can seem overwhelming. Break them down into smaller, actionable steps. For instance, if your goal is to transition to carbon neutrality within five years, the steps could include reducing energy use by 10% each year and offsetting emissions through verified carbon offset programs.

3. **Regular Review** : Sustainability goals should not be set in stone. Regularly review and assess your progress to ensure you're on track, and be flexible enough to adjust your goals based on new data or changes in your business environment.

Example : A solopreneur in the fashion industry may set a goal of transitioning to 100% sustainable fabrics within the next five years. The first step could be using 50% organic cotton in the next year, followed by increasing the percentage incrementally each year until they reach their goal.

9.2 Adapting to New Technologies and Innovations in Sustainability

As sustainability technologies and innovations evolve, so too should your business. Keeping up with new tools, materials, and processes will help you stay competitive and continue to reduce your environmental footprint. Here are key areas where technology is transforming sustainability for solopreneurs:

1. **Renewable Energy Advancements** : While solar panels and wind energy are common today, advancements in renewable energy storage, like **lithium-ion batteries** and **grid storage** , can help you optimize energy use. Keep an eye on these developments and consider upgrading your energy systems as these technologies become more affordable.

2. **Sustainable Materials** : New materials that are more sustainable and biodegradable are constantly being developed. For example, **mycelium** (mushroom-based packaging) and **plant-based plastics** are gaining popularity as alternatives to traditional materials.

3. **Digital Tools for Monitoring Impact** : New tools and apps are making it easier for businesses to track and reduce their environmental impact. For example, carbon

footprint calculators, supply chain monitoring platforms, and **AI-powered sustainability tools** can help you monitor and optimize every aspect of your operations.

4. **Circular Economy Platforms** : Platforms that support the circular economy are growing in popularity. These allow businesses to design products with longer life cycles, offering reuse, repair, and recycling options to customers. Consider how you can integrate these tools into your business model to keep your products in use longer.

9.3 Expanding Sustainability Practices as Your Business Grows

As your business grows, it's important that your sustainability practices scale with it. Growth should not come at the expense of your commitment to sustainability. In fact, scaling sustainability is essential to building a resilient business that can thrive in a future where consumers, governments, and industries increasingly demand eco-friendly practices.

Here's how to expand your sustainability practices as your business grows:

1. **Scaling Your Supply Chain** : If you expand into new markets, ensure that your supply chain remains as sustainable as possible. Work with suppliers that are committed to ethical practices and maintain transparency in their sourcing. As you grow, consider forming partnerships with organizations that specialize in ethical supply chain management.

2. **Integrating Sustainability into Business Expansion** : If you plan to open a new location or expand your product line, integrate sustainability into every aspect of that expansion. For example, when choosing a new workspace, prioritize buildings that meet **LEED (Leadership in Energy and Environmental Design)** certification standards or use renewable energy.

3. **Engage Your Growing Team** : As your business grows and you potentially bring on employees or collaborators, make sure they are aligned with your sustainability goals. Train your team on the importance of sustainability, and empower them to contribute to your efforts.

9.4 Case Study: A Solopreneur's Journey to Long-Term Sustainability

Julia started a small business designing eco-friendly home decor made from upcycled materials. As her business grew, she realized that sustainability would need to be central to her long-term strategy if she wanted to maintain her brand's integrity.

She began by setting ambitious goals: reducing her carbon emissions by 50% within five years and transitioning to using 100% renewable energy for her production processes. Julia invested in renewable energy credits to offset her emissions in the short term, and after two years of research, she installed solar panels at her workshop to power her production equipment.

As part of her long-term strategy, Julia also formed partnerships with ethical suppliers and created a **buy-back program** where customers could return products at the end of their life cycle to be refurbished, recycled, or reused. This allowed her to build a circular business model that not only minimized waste but also created customer loyalty by offering discounts on future purchases.

Julia's commitment to long-term sustainability ensured that her business grew without sacrificing its core values. By continuously assessing and adapting her sustainability strategy, she was able to scale her business responsibly while staying true to her mission.

9.5 Exercise: Creating a 3-5 Year Sustainability Roadmap

Now it's time to create your own long-term sustainability roadmap. This exercise will help you plan for the future and ensure that sustainability remains a core focus as your business grows.

1. **Set a Vision** : What do you want your business to look like in 3-5 years in terms of sustainability? Consider areas like energy consumption, waste reduction, supply chain transparency, and customer engagement.

2. **Identify Key Milestones** : Break down your long-term vision into smaller, achievable milestones. For example, in the first year, you might focus on reducing energy consumption by 10%, and in the third year, transition to 100% renewable energy sources.

3. **Plan for Growth** : How will you maintain sustainability as your business scales? Think about how your supply chain, team, and operations will need to evolve as your business grows.

4. **Measure and Adjust** : Set up a process for regularly reviewing your progress. Identify metrics to track, such as carbon emissions, energy usage, and waste reduction, and adjust your roadmap as needed based on these insights.

Conclusion of Chapter 9

Long-term sustainability planning is essential for building a resilient, responsible business that can adapt to future challenges and opportunities. By setting ambitious but achievable goals, staying informed about new technologies, and scaling your sustainability practices as your business grows, you'll position your brand as a leader in sustainability. Solopreneurs are uniquely suited to lead the charge toward a greener future by constantly evolving their practices and adapting to a rapidly changing world.

Chapter 12

Conclusion

Your Entrepreneurial Journey with Less Digital Noise

As you reach the end of this book, it's clear that sustainability is not just a buzzword or a passing trend; it's a **vital component** of how modern businesses must operate, especially for solopreneurs who want to lead with purpose and integrity. Throughout the chapters, you've learned how to integrate sustainable practices into every aspect of your business, from sourcing materials to reducing energy consumption, all the way to building meaningful relationships with eco-conscious consumers.

What sets you apart as a solopreneur is your ability to make intentional, values-driven decisions quickly and efficiently. Unlike large corporations bogged down by bureaucracy, you have the agility to implement sustainable practices and adapt to new challenges and opportunities as they arise. This ability is one of your greatest strengths and should be leveraged as you continue on your journey.

The Value of Long-Term Commitment

Sustainability is not a one-time initiative but a **long-term commitment** . The steps you take today—no matter how small—are laying the foundation for a business that will stand the test of time, not just because it's profitable, but because it aligns with the values of today's environmentally and socially conscious consumers.

Remember, sustainable business practices are a **journey** , not a destination. The path to sustainability will evolve as new technologies, regulations, and consumer expectations emerge. The key is to remain adaptable and willing to innovate as you grow. Your

sustainability roadmap will guide you, but your ability to reflect, adjust, and expand your efforts will keep you moving forward.

Reaping the Benefits of Sustainability

By incorporating the principles of sustainability into your business, you're not just reducing waste or lowering your energy bills—you're building a brand that resonates with consumers who prioritize **ethical, environmentally responsible businesses** . These consumers are loyal, vocal, and willing to support brands that align with their values. The sustainable steps you take today will help you forge deeper connections with your customers, attract new ones, and stand out in a crowded marketplace.

In addition to customer loyalty, you'll also gain **operational efficiency** , **cost savings** , and a stronger resilience against future challenges—whether they're financial, environmental, or regulatory. Sustainable practices position your business for long-term success while contributing to the greater good.

Take Action Today

As you close this book, you now have the tools and knowledge to take immediate action. Begin with the **small, achievable steps** outlined in these chapters, whether it's conducting an energy audit, switching to sustainable suppliers, or creating a green loyalty program for your customers. Over time, these small actions will build momentum, allowing you to implement more ambitious sustainability goals.

Sustainability is a continuous journey, and every step you take brings you closer to a business that is not only successful but also purposeful. You have the potential to create a ripple effect in your community, inspiring others to follow your lead. Together, we can make a real difference—one sustainable business at a time.

Final Call to Action

Your entrepreneurial journey with sustainability is just beginning. Continue to grow, adapt, and inspire others with your eco-conscious business practices. Embrace the future with confidence, knowing that you are contributing to a healthier planet and a better world for future generations.

Now is the time to make sustainability a core part of your business—take that first step and watch as it transforms both your business and the world around you.

The future of solopreneurship is sustainable—and you are leading the way.

Chapter 13

NOTES

Chapter 1: The Solopreneur's Unique Challenge in a Sustainable World

1. **Nielsen Global Responsibility Study** : This study offers insights into consumer attitudes toward sustainability and ethical brands. You can explore global market research reports for more data on how sustainability influences consumer behavior.

2. **Triple Bottom Line Framework** : A foundational concept that drives the balance between people, planet, and profit. Many articles, business journals, and management textbooks explain how the Triple Bottom Line applies to modern business practices.

3. **Small Business Sustainability** : Research how small businesses, including solopreneurs, can lead in adopting sustainable practices. Industry publications often provide case studies and practical examples of small businesses implementing sustainability.

Chapter 2: Setting the Foundation for a Sustainable Business

1. **SMART Goals for Sustainability** : Use business development resources or sustainability-focused organizations to learn more about setting SMART (Specific, Measurable, Achievable, Relevant, Time-bound) goals to drive sustainable change in your business.

2. **Sustainability Audits** : Many environmental agencies and business development organizations offer guides on how to conduct a sustainability audit for small businesses. These resources are helpful for identifying key areas to improve.

3. **Case Study: Implementing Sustainable Business Practices** : Small business associations and sustainability organizations often publish case studies that illustrate how businesses have successfully implemented sustainable frameworks and strategies.

Chapter 3: Sustainable Sourcing and Ethical Supply Chains

1. **Sustainable Supply Chains** : Business journals and sustainability reports often provide strategies to build ethical and eco-friendly supply chains. Look for resources on green supply chain management.

2. **Certifications for Sustainable Products** : Various certification bodies, such as Fair Trade, Organic, or FSC (Forest Stewardship Council), provide information on how their certifications verify ethical and sustainable sourcing practices.

3. **Circular Economy in Business** : Look for publications from environmental foundations that focus on the circular economy model, which emphasizes waste reduction, reuse, and recycling in business.

Chapter 4: Reducing Waste and Embracing Circular Economy Practices

1. **The Circular Economy** : Environmental and business innovation organizations often provide detailed explanations of the circular economy model, offering practical examples of how businesses can transition away from linear production models.

2. **Waste Reduction Strategies for Small Businesses** : Environmental protection agencies and business sustainability websites often feature practical guides for reducing waste, especially in small business settings.

3. **Upcycling in Business** : You can find examples and insights on how to implement upcycling as part of your business model through design and sustainability platforms.

Chapter 5: Energy Efficiency and Sustainable Business Practices

1. **Energy Efficiency in Small Businesses** : Many utility companies and government organizations offer resources for improving energy efficiency in businesses, including incentive programs for adopting energy-saving technologies.

2. **Renewable Energy Options for Small Businesses** : Research publications and energy service providers often offer resources on adopting solar, wind, and other renewable energy solutions for small and home-based businesses.

3. **Conducting an Energy Audit** : Numerous guides are available from energy service providers and environmental organizations that explain how to conduct an energy audit and identify areas for improvement in energy efficiency.

Chapter 6: Sustainable Marketing and Ethical Branding

1. **Sustainable Marketing Strategies** : Marketing publications and sustainability-focused business resources offer strategies for marketing sustainability effectively, helping businesses avoid the pitfalls of greenwashing.

2. **Avoiding Greenwashing** : Business ethics resources often discuss how to avoid greenwashing, providing insights on how businesses can maintain integrity in their sustainability claims.

3. **Brand Transparency in Sustainability** : Many business journals and corporate transparency advocates provide case studies and frameworks for how brands can build trust through open communication about their sustainability practices.

Chapter 7: Sustainable Finance: Budgeting for a Greener Business

1. **Sustainable Finance for Small Businesses** : Explore resources from finance publications or organizations focused on sustainable investing to better understand how small businesses can align their financial practices with sustainability.

2. **Calculating the ROI of Sustainability** : Look for business studies and sustainability reports that explain how businesses can measure the financial benefits of sustainable practices, such as energy savings and waste reduction.

3. **Cost-Effective Sustainable Solutions** : Various business and sustainability websites offer lists of affordable ways small businesses can begin integrating sustainability, from energy-saving tips to eco-friendly materials.

Chapter 8: Building Customer Loyalty Through Sustainability

1. **Consumer Preferences and Sustainability** : Consumer research studies from global market research companies provide insights into how sustainability influences customer loyalty and purchasing decisions.

2. **Green Loyalty Programs** : Many marketing publications and loyalty program experts discuss how businesses can create customer loyalty programs centered around eco-friendly initiatives.

3. **Building Customer Engagement Around Sustainability** : Look for business and marketing strategy guides that focus on engaging eco-conscious consumers through transparent and consistent sustainability messaging.

Chapter 9: Long-Term Sustainability Planning for Solopreneurs

1. **Long-Term Sustainability Planning** : Government and business sustainability organizations often provide guides on how to develop a long-term sustainability strategy for businesses of all sizes.

2. **Sustainability and Technological Innovation** : Many business and technology innovation reports cover how advances in sustainability technologies—such as renewable energy and circular economy tools—can benefit small businesses.

3. **Scaling Sustainability as Your Business Grows** : Research from business associations and sustainability consultants often addresses how businesses can maintain their commitment to sustainability while scaling their operations.

These references will help guide deeper research and support your sustainability efforts as a solopreneur. Each chapter touches on critical areas for solopreneurs looking to integrate sustainability into their operations while creating long-term value for their customers and the planet.

Chapter 14

AUTHOR

SUFI is a passionate advocate for sustainable business practices and mindful entrepreneurship. With over 20 years of hands-on experience in social welfare and counseling, SUFI brings a unique blend of **compassion, business acumen, and a deep understanding of human psychology** to the world of solopreneurs. His life's work revolves around empowering individuals and marginalized communities, helping them rise above challenges through sustainable practices and innovative business models.

As a public speaker, SUFI is known for delivering **inspiring, thought-provoking talks** that challenge conventional wisdom and motivate audiences to take action. His ability to connect deeply with people from all walks of life makes him a powerful voice in the sustainability movement. SUFI's talks leave a lasting impact, encouraging entrepreneurs to not only focus on profits but also to consider their social and environmental responsibilities.

As an author, SUFI weaves together **real-life experiences, practical advice, and profound insights** on how solopreneurs can build businesses that align with their values, while also making a positive impact on the world. His writing is not just about sharing knowledge—it's about igniting meaningful change in how business is conducted. Through his work, SUFI invites solopreneurs to embrace sustainability, not only as a business strategy but as a **way of life** , encouraging them to build a future where business success and social responsibility go hand in hand.

In his book *Sustainable Solopreneurship* , SUFI combines his passion for **ethical living, social impact, and environmental sustainability** , offering a clear roadmap for entrepreneurs looking to make a lasting difference in their industries and the world.

www.ingramcontent.com/pod-product-compliance
Lightning Source LLC
Chambersburg PA
CBHW070412230526
45471CB00006B/2771